⊕ AN OBSERVER'S GUIDE

Making Clothes—Stage 2

The Sewing Machine

Toni Naldrett

Illustrations by Barbara Firth

GW00776493

FREDERICK WARNE

Published by Frederick Warne (Publishers) Ltd, London, 1982
©Frederick Warne (Publishers) Ltd, 1982

Imperial and metric measurements are used throughout the book.
Choose either the metric or imperial system and stick to it throughout
the project—changing from one system to the other will lead to
inaccuracy and mistakes.

ISBN 0 7232 2891 4

Filmset and printed in Great Britain
by BAS Printers Limited, Over Wallop, Hampshire

Contents

Introduction

A new sewing machine costs a great deal of money. It is regrettable that many dressmakers not only under-use their machines, but also produce inexpert sewing! This is a waste of both their time and capital investment.

This book first of all describes the different kinds of sewing machine available and advises on the best model for your needs. Working in conjunction with your own sewing machine instruction book, the book then guides you through the process of familiarizing yourself with your machine. It also shows you how to speed up the routine processes when machining. If you have never, ever used a sewing machine do read the special section on how to make the machine actually sew!

Having achieved these first steps, you can go on to explore ways of using your new-found confidence on the sewing machine. Many dressmakers use their sewing machines in conjunction with a range of sewing methods to join their garments together. It is possible to sew clothes together completely by machine. This speeds up the work and adds strength to the construction. Do please remember that although the words 'clothes', 'garments' and 'dressmaking' are used throughout the book, your sewing machine is an invaluable aid in other creative projects for you and your family and home. The pattern catalogues and magazines are bursting with fresh, lively ideas for things to make. By following this book's advice, you will improve your standard of workmanship and gain more time to enjoy many other aspects of sewing.

Please note that in all illustrations the wrong side of the fabric is represented by shading.

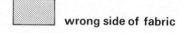 wrong side of fabric

Phase 1

Choosing a sewing machine

Buying a sewing machine can be an expensive and confusing business these days. There are a bewildering variety of makes and each model seems to have extra functions which you have never heard of. Whichever machine you choose, try to buy the best you can afford. Quality will pay you back every time.

Which machine for you?

There are three basic types of machine:

HAND MACHINES

These are incredibly strong, well built and very simple in function. They will sew in a straight line and are operated by rotating the wheel manually. Our grandmothers managed very well with them. They are excellent for a real beginner who might feel hesitant at the speed of an electric machine, or who is wary of the high capital investment of an electric machine, being unsure of her ability and the enjoyment of dressmaking. These old machines are also a good, safe way to interest children in sewing—enabling them to make 'real clothes' for themselves. A wide range of extra feet is available—rufflers, pleaters, roll hemmers and cording feet— giving greater scope to your dressmaking. If you decide to buy a hand machine, always look for a reconditioned model, or have your proposed purchase checked by an expert before buying.

ELECTRIC MACHINES

Straight-stitch electric models are really little more than hand machines with electric motors added. They have the facility to stitch backwards easily which is more useful, but these machines will not give the full range of stitches and finishes that are needed for modern, stretch-knit fabrics. So if you are investing in a new sewing machine, save up some more money and look around for a swing-needle machine.

SWING-NEEDLE MACHINES

The next great leap forward in the life history of the domestic sewing machine was the introduction of the swing-needle or zig-zag machine for the home user. These machines stitch not only backwards and forwards but also from side to side. Some earlier types of swing-needle machines have only two positions—centre and to one side—but most modern machines have three positions—centre, left and right. This 'zig-zag' stitch opens up whole new areas of sewing—machine button-holes, stretch stitching for modern knit fabrics, neater seam finishing and effortless embroidery to decorate your creations. These machines come in three variations:

Plain zig-zig These machines do straight and zig-zag stitches as well as simple button-holing and seam finishing, but they depend on manual control for altering stitch width and length. This means that producing simple embroidery patterns and fancy stitching is dependent on your skill in using the controls. This simple model is rarely produced these days but can be bought as a reconditioned machine for the infrequent dressmaker.

Semi-automatic The semi-automatic, swing-needle machine is the most popular model produced for the home market. It gives the dressmaker a range of straight, zig-zig and stretch stitches necessary for modern sewing. It has the capacity to make machine button-holes without demanding too much manual skill and a small but useful range of embroidery stitches that can be produced by the machine alone. Your choice of machine in this range really depends on an assessment of your needs. The tiny portable models are ideal for the infrequent dressmaker or one whose sewing and storage space is limited. If you plan to sew for your home and family your choice would be the larger, heavy duty machines. Many swing-needle machines now have a choice of sewing surfaces. The flat table is used for most machining but can be removed to enable you to work with the 'free arm'. This narrow circular arm is so useful for smaller chores.

Fully-automatic As the name implies, these machines give all the

6

services of a semi-automatic model but automatically. Button-holes are completed by the machine—the sewer does not have to turn the garment or adjust the stitches. The range of embroidery stitches is also much wider. All this splendour, however, costs much more than the semi-automatic machine! You must be a really dedicated dressmaker to justify the extra cost.

ELECTRONIC AND COMPUTER MACHINES

The sewing machine industry is constantly advancing with modern technology and improving its designs. The micro-chip has, of course, entered the field and is incorporated in some machines. Most of these advances are in simplifying the many processes a sewing machine can perform providing easier stitch selection, more sensitive foot control and a wider range of decorative stitches. But the basic design of the sewing machine, its shape and mechanics, remains the same and will do so while clothes construction and fabrics continue as we know them.

MACHINES FOR THE DISABLED

There is a wide range of adaptations available to assist people with various disabilities. Ask your retailer or local association for the disabled about these.

Where to buy your machine

Sewing machines seem to be acquired in all sorts of ways. You may be given one, or buy it from a friend. Advertisements in local newspapers or newsagents' windows are another source. If you buy your machine in any of these ways, please have it checked by your local sewing machine retailer or service agent. It is a great help to make a friend of your local sewing machine retailer, especially if you intend to buy a new or reconditioned machine from the shop. They should be able to give you the back up of service, lessons and advice afterwards. It is often wiser to pay more in the beginning for a machine from a good, helpful retailer, than get a price reduction and no after-sales service.

TWELVE POINTS TO CONSIDER WHEN BUYING YOUR MACHINE

1   Is the machine easy to set up for sewing and light enough for you to carry it in its storage case?
2   Is it easy to thread up the needle and to rewind the bobbin? DO try this for yourself—the demonstrator is paid to make it look easy!

3 Does the bobbin drop simply into its sewing position in the machine?

4 Are there variable speeds for motor control?

5 How noisy is the motor when it is running?

6 How comfortable and sensitive is the foot control to use?

7 Have you the choice of flat working table and free arm?

8 How easy is it to change the foot and what choice of feet is included in the basic price?

9 How simple is the machine to clean and oil? Can it be reassembled easily?

10 Are there country-wide service agents?

11 Is the instruction book comprehensive and clearly written? This is very important!

12 How wide is the range of accessories? Is there a varied range of embroidery stitches and a selection of feet for sewing leather, quilting and other fabrics?

Phase 2

A working knowledge of your machine

However experienced a machinist you are, the process of getting to know a new machine takes time. It is best undertaken on your own, in peace and quiet. To the beginner, this shining monster may seem fearsome—remember it is only a machine and that *you* are in control of *it*! Each machine has different placements for its controls so this section must be practised with the machine's own manual to hand. Each of the next stages has a 'Learner's test' for you to pass. This will help you to achieve control of your machine. Whenever you use your machine, make sure that you are sitting comfortably and that your chair is at the right height in relation to your surface—backache spoils dressmaking.

Learner's test I

Open up the machine case and put the machine on your work table. Don't bother to connect the electricity for this part. Find the right paragraph in this book for your machine—hand, swing-needle etc—and with your own sewing machine instruction book beside you, identify all the parts.

HAND OR STRAIGHT-STITCH ELECTRIC MACHINE

1 *Wheel and handle* (right of machine) Attach handle as shown in instruction book to enable you to operate the machine.
2 *Handwheel release* (sometimes called balance-wheel-stop-motion screw!) This frees the needle to wind the bobbin.
3 *Bobbin winder* Just find out where this is. (Don't bother with how to use it for the moment.)
4 *Thread spool pin* This holds the thread reel while you are sewing. It is usually on top of the machine.

5 *Pressure regulator* Some machines don't have this, so don't worry. It should be on the top of the machine at the opposite end to the spool pin.

6 *Thread take-up lever* This moves up and down, pulling the thread off the reel and through the tension guide.

7 *Thread guide or wire* The location of this can vary according to the make of the machine.

8 *Tension discs* These are circular discs with an adjustable screw holding them in place. To alter the upper thread tension: tighten the screw to increase the thread tension, or loosen the screw to lessen tension. Sometimes there are numbers on the discs to help you judge the tension accurately.

9 *Thread guides* These are other thread guides or wires. You will usually find these down the needle side of the machine.

10 *Needle* That's obvious!

11 *Needle change screw* Find this at the top of the needle.

12 *Presser foot lever* At the rear of the machine is a lever that goes up and down to operate the needle presser foot. It must be *down* when you sew.

13 *Needle presser foot* Easy to find! This surrounds the needle. Also find the screw with which you can change the foot. This needle presser foot must also be *down* before you sew. It is operated by the presser foot lever (**12**)

14 *Foot remover* This can be a screw or lever system. Practise to be able to remove and change the foot in at least 10 seconds.

15 *Thread cutter* Be careful how you search for this—it's sharp! It is usually just behind the needle, for ease of use.

16 *Throat plate* This is just below the needle. The small round hole enables the needle to go through to pick up the bobbin thread below. The sharp teeth move back and forth to take the fabric away from the needle.

17 *Slide plate or bobbin cover* Next to the throat plate, is a sliding plate which opens up to show the bobbin case. Always sew with this closed, otherwise your fabric will get caught in the workings below. On some models this can be below the throat plate and swing outwards to show the bobbin case.

18 *Bobbin case* The threaded bobbin fits into this case. The bobbin tension spring is located around the outside edge. Can you find the screw that alters the tension?

19 *Bobbin ejector* Some machines have this useful lever to raise the bobbin out of its tight case.

20 *Stitch length regulator* This is usually found on the right of the machine front. It can either be a knob that winds in and out to lengthen or shorten stitch, or it may be a lever that moves.

21 *Reverse stitch regulator* This will only be found on the straight-stitch electric machine. Learn how to use it later on—it is a very important aid to quick dressmaking.

22 *Electric foot pedal* This is the foot control operating an electric machine. It can plug in separately or together with the mains lead, or in some older models it may be permanently attached to the machine.

Now that you have identified the principal parts of your machine, continue to study them and learn their positions and names until you feel confident enough to try the first test.

CLOSE your sewing machine instruction book and run through the list in Learner's test IA. If you score under 12, go back and relearn the parts!

L-TEST IA—for hand or straight-stitch electric machines
Identify the following parts on your machine:

1	Wheel and handle	12	Presser foot lever
2	Handwheel release	13	Needle presser foot
3	Bobbin winder	14	Foot remover
4	Thread spool pin	15	Thread cutter
5	Pressure regulator	16	Throat plate
6	Thread take-up lever	17	Slide plate or bobbin cover
7	Thread guide or wire	18	Bobbin case
8	Tension discs	19	Bobbin ejector
9	Thread guides	20	Stitch length regulator
10	Needle	21	Reverse stitch regulator
11	Needle change screw	22	Electric foot pedal

SWING-NEEDLE MACHINES

Follow the list for hand/straight-stitch machines of the first 22 principal parts to identify. Then look for the following new parts—making particular reference to your own machine's instruction book. It would be impossible, in this book, to write a description to cover all the designs of modern sewing machines. Many models have different positions on the machine's body for the parts, some use alternative names and others do not possess some parts at all!

1–22 as hand/straight-stitch machines

23 *Stitch width selector* This is used particularly for selecting the width of the zig-zag stitch.

24 *Needle position selector* Not all machines have this. It will move the needle to left, centre or right.

25 *Pattern selector* The method of selection and range of stitches varies tremendously. This selector is usually worked in conjunction with the controls for stitch width and length for greater variety.

26 *Automatic button-holer* This is a feature of some fully-automatic machines.

27 *Drop feed control* This enables you to lower the teeth in the throat plate to allow the needle free range of stitching for darning and some embroideries.

28 *Sewing table* The large, flat surface around the needle to sew on. It clips on and off to reveal the free arm in the middle. (Can you remove this in 5 seconds?)

29 *Free arm* This narrow arm, which houses the bobbin, has become a valuable modification of sewing machine design as it simplifies the smaller, fiddly areas of garments such as sleeves and cuffs.

30 *Variable motor speed switch* This has many other names and different positions on various machines. It is of great help to novice dressmakers in slowing the speed of the motor.

31 *Sewing machine light switch* You must find this—to save eye strain.

Having learnt the names and locations of the parts of your sewing machine, try the following Learner's test 1B *without* your own machine instruction book to help. Anyone scoring under 22 should relearn the lot!

L-TEST 1 B—for swing-needle machines
Identify the following parts of your machine:

1	Wheel	**7**	Thread guide or wire
2	Handwheel release	**8**	Tension discs
3	Bobbin winder	**9**	Thread guides
4	Thread spool pin	**10**	Needle
5	Pressure regulator	**11**	Needle change screw
6	Thread take-up lever	**12**	Presser foot lever

13	Needle presser foot	23	Stitch width selector
14	Foot remover	24	Needle position selector
15	Thread cutter	25	Pattern selector
16	Throat plate	26	Automatic button-holer
17	Slide plate or bobbin cover	27	Drop feed control
18	Bobbin case	28	Sewing table
19	Bobbin ejector	29	Free arm
20	Stitch length regulator	30	Variable motor speed switch
21	Reverse stitch regulator	31	Sewing machine light switch
22	Electric foot pedal		

Learner's test II

This test is divided into four timed operations. Do them first with the help of your instruction book then *close* it and test yourself without it.

L-TEST II A— *5-minute set-up*

1 Remove machine from case.
2 Plug in electric machine.
3 Check that you have the correct needle and presser foot for your sewing project (see page 23).
4 Thread up bobbin and place in sewing position.

Figure 1

5 Thread your needle and raise bobbin thread, by hand. Lay upper and lower threads neatly behind the foot as illustrated (Figure 1).

13

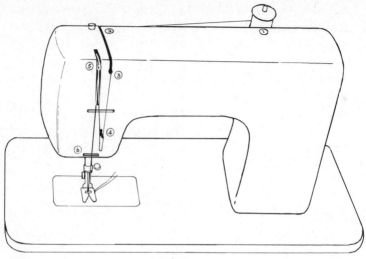

Figure 2

Quick tip

To help remember the sequence of needle threading, buy some tiny adhesive numbers at your office stationers and stick numbers on each position in the threading sequence—then follow the numbers (Figure 2).

L-TEST II B—*3-minute pack-up*

1   Unplug electric machine.
2   Dismantle machine.
3   Pack machine in case.

This pack-up operation does not include cleaning and oiling your machine. This process is described in Phase 5 and should be done after completing each garment.

L-TEST II C—*30-second needle change*

1   Take out broken, blunt or unsuitable needle. (Always have the right tool for this near your machine.)
2   Slide in replacement needle, making sure that the flat side of the needle is in the right position for your machine. (Check this with the mirror of a powder compact by sliding it under the needle opening to see where the flat side must lie.)
3   Tighten needle into place and rethread.

14

1 Take out empty bobbin and place in winding position.
2 Thread up and wind on thread.
3 Re-insert bobbin into machine and pull up bobbin thread after rethreading machine.

When you have successfully completed these four operations in the necessary times and from memory, proceed on to the next section.

Starting to sew

This section is really designed for those who have never handled a sewing machine before, but even the most proficient dressmakers will find techniques that need improving or relearning.

    Many beginner dressmakers find themselves sitting in front of the sewing machine without the first idea of how to make it sew. If this is you, take heart and follow these steps:

1 Thread up the needle and bobbin as discussed in L-test II A.
2 Place the edge of a large scrap of folded fabric under the needle presser foot.
3 Before sewing, the real beginner will find it easier to lower the needle into the fabric, at exactly the spot where you will begin, by turning the hand wheel.
4 Lower the presser foot by means of the lever at the back of the machine. This lever can be called the needle presser lever or needle lever.
5 While keeping one hand on the fabric scrap, *gently* turn the handle on the wheel away from you, or press the foot pedal with the ball of your foot. It helps to be able to rock from the ball to the heel of your foot for greatest control.
6 The needle is dancing up and down, stitching your first seam! If you feel the fabric is running away with you, don't pull it towards you, this will not slow it down but bend your needle instead. The control of the machine lies in your hand on the wheel or your foot on the presser pedal. Ease your foot back and the speed will slacken, just like the accelerator of a car.

Practise to gain your confidence and then go on to test III.

Learner's test III

No timings here—confidence and good, neat work are more important than speed, which will come naturally with practice.

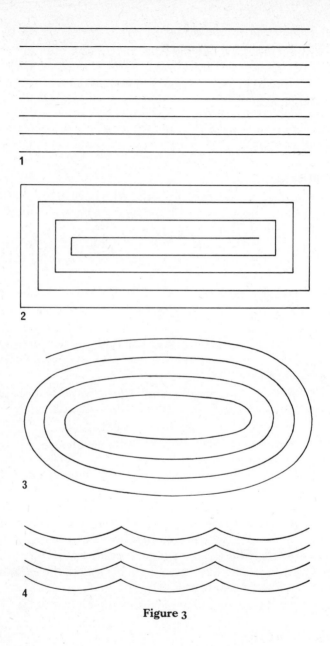

Figure 3

Draw the patterns illustrated (Figure 3) with felt-tipped pen on to sheets of paper or fusible interfacing. An ideal size to draw the test patterns is 15 cm (6 in) long by 7.5 cm (3 in) wide. Draw several of each pattern. It is more economical not to thread up your machine with sewing thread as the needle will puncture the paper and you can see your progress by holding up the finished exercises to the light. Find out how the different pressures of your foot, or turn of your hand, will alter the speed of your sewing. Start at a slow speed. It is better to be careful and accurate, than rapid and wobbly. If your machine has a fast and slow speed switch, use the slow one to help you.

L-TEST III A—*Straight lines*

Once you have sewn several really good straight lines, start to practise finishing off the last stitch with your needle *in* the exercise, just by control. Don't cheat and use your hand wheel if your machine is electric. The ability to do this will help you in the next test which is turning corners. Practise pattern 1.

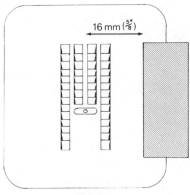

16 mm ($\frac{5}{8}$)

Figure 4

Quick tip

It may help you to use the straight lines marked on the throat plate as guidance. If these don't exist on your own machine, place a strip of adhesive tape 16 mm ($\frac{5}{8}$ in) to the right of the needle (Figure 4). This is the width of seam normally used.

17

L-TEST III B—*Turning corners* (Figure 5)

1 Always finish at a corner with your needle *in* the exercise.

2 Keep your foot poised over the foot control and raise the presser foot.

3 Turn the exercise until the un-sewn line lies directly under the needle and then lower the presser foot.

4 Continue stitching down the line. Practise pattern 2

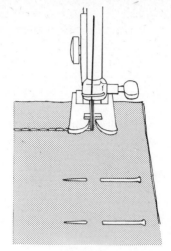

L-TEST III C—*Stitching curves*

Figure 5

Real control is needed here! Work your way gently around the exercise to begin with. Easing your foot pressure on the control will give you time to turn gently as you go. If you have ever listened to the machine noise that a professional machinist makes, you will notice the short, sharp bursts of speed that changing foot pressure produces, when working on a complicated process.
Practise patterns 3 and 4.

Now the shining monster is half way to being tamed. If you can accomplish the previous exercises neatly and confidently, you are ready to begin a long, happy and creative friendship with your machine.

Tips and techniques for sewing on your machine

The final part of this phase tells you about the everyday sewing techniques you will use each time you sew. Practise on each new project you undertake and you will improve the quality of your sewing and save yourself time and trouble.

1 Buy a little extra fabric for stitching and pressing trials for each new project. It is better to be safe and experiment before starting than to be sorry with an unsatisfactory garment at the end. You will find that the lighter the fabric the smaller the stitch length will need to be, but always experiment as the results will guide your choice. As a guide, an average stitch length for a medium-weight fabric would be 10 stitches to 2.5 cm (1 in).

18

Straight stitch for all normal sewing on natural fabrics.

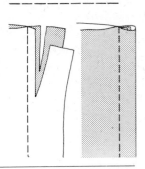

French seam for sheer fabrics and lingerie. First stitch seam with WRONG sides facing, trim, back turn to enclose seam and stitch right sides facing.

Flat felled seam for extra tough strong clothes. First stitch seam with WRONG sides facing, trim away one seam edge and press whole seam to one side. Turn and top stitch as shown.

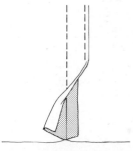

Zig-zag stitch for most stretch, man-made fabrics. Either of these stitches is good for elastic or super-stretch fabrics.

Stretch stitch version of flat felled seam for stretch sportswear. With RIGHT sides together first sew seam, using zig-zag stitch, press open and stitch over open seam with wider zig-zag stitch.

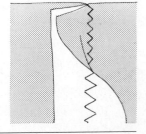

Flat joined seam is best for elastic underwear. Use one of the stitches recommended above for elastic or the one shown. Lay the two fabrics 6 mm ($\frac{1}{4}$ in) on top of each other and sew each edge as illustrated.

19

Neatening This is a very good seam finish for cottons and light natural fabrics. It does need practice to turn 3 mm ($\frac{1}{8}$ in) under as you sew, but you can press the edge first for accuracy.

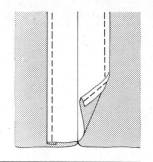

Pinking shears make a quick neat seam finish. This finish is suitable for wool or synthetics. Stitch a line of straight stitches then pink close to the stitch. It can be done either pressed open or with the two seams together for a narrow seam.

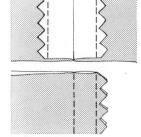

Zig-zag stitch provides a basic seam finish. It is important to make sure the stitch lies on the edge of the seam to lock the fraying fabric threads in place. This is suitable for all kinds of fabrics.

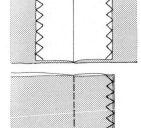

Automatic seam finishing These stitches are found only on semi- and fully-automatic machines. They will join the seam and finish the edge in one operation! Very speedy, but not really recommended for clothes that are given rough treatment.

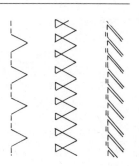

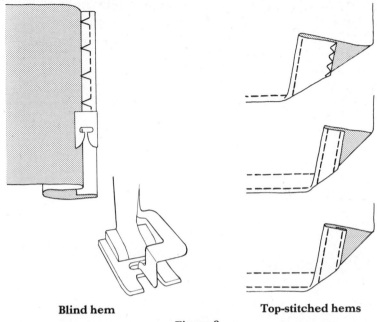

Blind hem **Top-stitched hems**

Figure 8

4 BASIC HEMS (Figure 8)

Blind hem This stitch is done with a special blind-hemmer foot which is not essential but aids accuracy. If this foot is not available use your normal zig-zag foot. Fold the hem as shown and press lightly to hold. Set the machine to the stitch illustrated, position the hem under the foot, to start just after a seam. The zig-zag stitch must only catch a few threads of the top fabric. The heavier fabrics, particularly household furnishings, show less mark. Press well after sewing.

Top-stitched hem These narrow top-stitched hems are ideal for knits and light cotton fabrics. Trim the hem to 16 mm ($\frac{5}{8}$ in) and finish the bottom edge either by zig-zag stitch or by turning under 6 mm ($\frac{1}{4}$ in). Press hem allowance into place and proceed to stitch as illustrated.

5 *Always* start stitching with both bobbin and needle threads lying neatly behind the foot (see Figure 1). This will give a smooth start and prevent the threads tangling.

6 Use your machine to finish off your stitching (Figure 9)—there is no need to tie the ends laboriously by hand. Start your stitching 12 mm ($\frac{1}{2}$ in) in from the edge. Reverse to the edge then proceed forwards until the seam or dart is complete, and finish off by reversing 12 mm ($\frac{1}{2}$ in) at the end. If there is no reverse facility on your machine, start to work 12 mm ($\frac{1}{4}$ in) in, and sew *towards* the end of the seam. Then lift the presser foot, turn the work around and proceed to sew as usual.

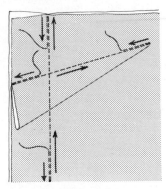

Figure 9

7 Snip your loose threads as you go. A forest of dangling threads is disheartening to clear up when the project is finished.

8 To produce a smooth, even, trouble-free seam of machine stitches, the correct needle is vital. Most fabrics are happy with a normal sharp needle, the choice of diameter being your only problem—the finer the fabric, the slimmer the needle. The problems of sewing synthetic stretch-knit fabrics can be helped by using a ball-point needle. This rounded needle slides between the threads whereas a normal sharp needle can catch and split the fibres, and make the seam pucker. A machine needle will quickly blunt, scratch, burr, and bend, all of which interferes with good quality stitching. It is wise to change your needle for each new project. Consult figure 10 and the table on page 23 for the correct choice of needle.

9 Once you have the correct needle in your machine, what about the thread to put through it? Your fabric will require a complimentary thread (see page 23). Natural fibres are happiest with mercerized cotton, no 40 or no 50. These numbers refer to the thread size—the higher the number the finer the thread—no 40

Thread and needle guide

The following chart is a guide to choosing the correct needle and thread for your fabric. There are too many individual materials to name, so a few have been given to help identify the weight of your own fabric.

Natural fibres	Machine needle	Thread
Lightweights: crêpes, lawns, wools, silks, cottons	*Sharp*: 11/80 to 14/90	fine, mercerized cotton or pure silk (for silk)
Medium weights: suitings cords, velvets, gaberdines, linens, cottons	14/90	mercerized cotton no 50
Heavyweights: coatings, linen union, denim, sailcloth	16/100	mercerized cotton no 40
Synthetic fibres *Lightweights*: nets, sheers, lingerie fabrics, knits	*Ball point*: 9/70 to 11/80	Synthetic thread, (these are all about the same size)
Medium weights: double knits, polyester jerseys, heavy nylons, stretch knits, polyester sheetings	11/80 to 14/90	synthetic thread
Heavyweights: bonded knits	16/100	synthetic thread
Leather	*Wedge shaped*: 11/80 to 14/90	mercerized cotton no 50 or no 40
PVC	*Sharp*: 16/100	,,
Button-holes and top-stitching For *all* fabrics	Same needle as rest of project	polyester button-hole thread, or double the thread in use

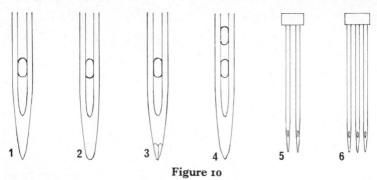

Figure 10

1 Normal sewing needle for natural fibres, 2 Ball point needle for manmade fibres, 3 Wedge-shaped needle for sewing leather, 4 Double eyed needle for machine tacking, 5 Double needle for pintucking, 6 Treble needle for narrower pintucks

being a heavy-duty size. If you are lucky enough to be working in pure silk, enjoy the added luxury of real silk thread for that extra good seam finish. Again, the higher the number the finer the thread—from 100/3 for seams down to 30/3 which is button-hole weight. Synthetic fibres need synthetic threads. Choose from 100 per cent polyester or Terylene—seam weight or heavier top-stitch, button-hole thread. When matching your colours of thread to fabric, choose the reel a shade *darker* than the predominant colour of your fabric. The single thread will appear lighter in the work. With the increased use of your machine you will need more thread so always buy at least two reels for a simple garment.

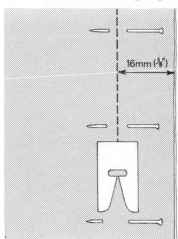

Figure 11

24

10 It is not necessary to tack before you machine (Figure 11). If you pin each piece of sewing together with the pins lying *horizontally* across the seam line you can then machine over the pins, as the presser foot will glide straight over the obstruction. What a time saver! If you do feel the need to tack before sewing because you are unsure of the fit of a new paper pattern, and you have a swing-needle machine, fit the special tacking needle. Again, this will save you time. These methods are described in more detail later.

Figure 12

11 Once you have threaded up and are ready to go, the first step in your project construction is frequently STAY STITCHING. Many sewers disgregard this stage, but in doing so they add to their problems later with wavy necklines, armholes and areas cut on the bias grain. Loosely woven materials and jersey knits are most affected by this stretching problem. Judge for yourself the necessity for stay stitching the fabric—let your fingers tell you! A line of straight stitches set at normal stitch length, sewn within the seam allowance, will hold these stretchy areas in place. Follow Figure 12 for the correct stitching direction. If you find it difficult to remember which way to go, make a rough sketch of the diagram and keep it near your machine.

12 *Unpicking*—yes it does happen! But, with the following method it is much less messy than before. This method has three advantages—no more ripped seams or accidental cuts in fabric; no more tiny, tiresome ends of thread to pull out; and greater accuracy, as you can judge exactly where and how much you wish

25

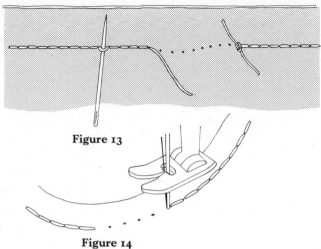

Figure 13

Figure 14

to unpick. Take a large darning needle—a pin would do, but a large needle is easier to hold for long periods of time. Start by *gently* easing out a stitch with the needle on the BOBBIN thread side and snip it in half. Now work every third or fourth stitch out. Some bobbin tensions are looser so that 6–10 stitches at a time can be pulled. Cut the loose thread as it becomes too long to pull through with comfort. After completing the unpicking, turn the work over and pull out the needle thread in one long piece.

This unpicking method can also be used as a first step in the following easy way of rescuing machine stitching mistakes. Snip the bobbin thread in the middle of the 'wobbly' area and pull stitches back to the good machining (Figure 13). Pull the NEEDLE thread through to the underneath and knot it together with the bobbin thread. Do this on the underside of seams that show, such as top-stitching. Now gently guide the machine needle in to the base hole of the last stitch, lower the presser foot into sewing position and restitch the 'wobbled' area (Figure 14). Repeat the pulling through of the needle thread to knot with bobbin thread at each end of sewing and you have an invisible and strong mistake saver!

13 At some point in the sewing of your garment you will probably have to do some gathering (Figure 15). Plan to do all sections at once—this saves altering stitch lengths continually. Set the machine to STRAIGHT SEWING on the longest stitch length. Two

26

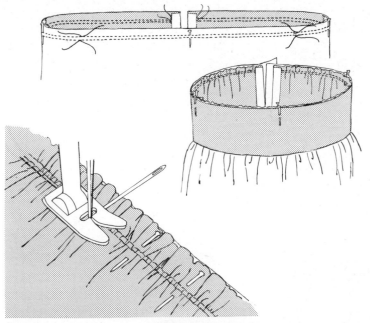

Figure 15

lines of long stitches set close together inside the 16 mm ($\frac{5}{8}$ in) seam allowance will give an easily manageable gather. Pull the bobbin thread gently and the fabric will bunch together. If you have a great deal of surplus to draw up—such as a skirt waist—it will be easier for you to stitch the two rows in lengths of 30 cm (12 in). When attaching the gathered area to its partner, divide each piece (gathered and straight) equally into halves or quarters, according to the amount of fabric, and then match these balance points together. Ease the surplus in evenly between these balance points. When machining the gathering on to its partner, work with the gathering on top and guide the bulk under the needle presser foot with your unpicking needle. This will give you extra hold to maintain even gathering especially on slippery fabric. This is the basic machine gathering method. For more decorative and time-saving ideas see Phase 4.

14 This next sewing method has the colourful title 'stitch in a ditch' (Figure 16). It is a way to save time-consuming hand sewing usually necessary to hold facings, collar necks, cuffs and bindings in place. Set the machine to straight stitching at a medium stitch

27

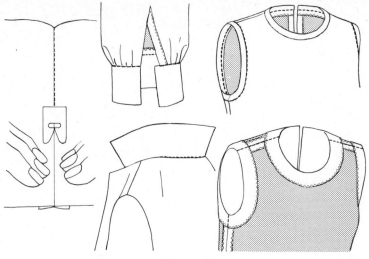

Figure 16

length. Machine on the *right* side of the garment in the hollow or 'ditch' formed by the slight curve of the seam. It is easier to find the ditch if you flatten the curve with your fingers before you sew. When you have finished machining the seam will roll together and the stitching becomes almost invisible.

15 One of the hardest sewing manoeuvres is that of joining opposite curves and corners (Figure 17). They often appear as part of design detail, as in princess seams (a) or set-in yokes (b), so it is worth taking extra care and doing them well. Otherwise your new dressmaking project will look very home-made! Start by stay stitching as illustrated. It is important to use small stitches for extra strength and to sew just within the seam line. Clip to the stay-stitching line as shown. Put a pin along the line of stitching if you are worried about snipping through it. Now machine as shown, always with the clipped edges facing you, to enable you to control the match of the two edges by opening or closing the clips. If your right-hand fingers obscure the operation try using the unpicking needle as used in no **13** on gathering.

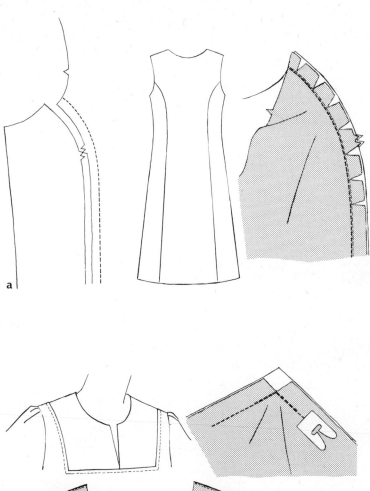

a

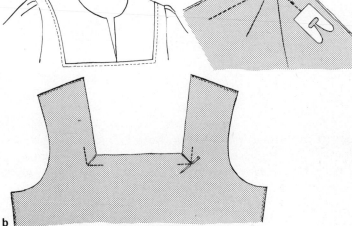

b

Figure 17

Phase 3

Machining technique

This phase contains more techniques for improving the speed and efficiency of your dressmaking.

BELTS

By making the 'turning-through gap' in the middle of a self-fabric belt, the belt ends can be machined neatly to finish with the seam either at the bottom or in the middle as shown in Figure 18. Use a fat wooden knitting needle to help turn through.

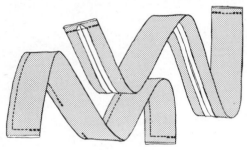

Figure 18

BINDINGS

The stitch-in-a-ditch method of finishing is excellent for bias-strip binding. Turn to neckline illustration in Phase 2, tips and techniques **14**. Remember to stretch the bias strip slightly as you machine and the finished binding will be flatter as a result.

BUTTONS

This chore can only be done by swing-needle machines. Figure 19 shows which foot to use. Be sure to adjust the zig-zag stitch width

Figure 19

to fit the holes—test by rotating the hand wheel as the needle might break if you use the electric foot pedal. A shank can be accommodated by placing a darning needle between the two holes.

CHIFFON

To make a really professional job of machining chiffon you must have a new, fine (no 11), sharp needle and an equally fine thread. Look for a synthetic thread that is recommended for sewing all fabrics as these are finer than mercerized cotton. If you are working on pure silk chiffon use pure silk thread. The beautiful, light, floating quality of chiffon has its drawbacks when trying to machine stitch. To prevent snags and puckering, try sewing on top of a layer of tissue paper. The paper is easily removed afterwards by gently tearing it away from the stitches. You will find that a fine french seam is the best finish to use.

CUFFS

Button cuffs (Figure 20)

1   Prepare cuff with interfacing and pressed hem. Stitch to sleeve, right sides together, as shown.

2   Fold up and stitch. Trim seams, mitre corners and turn through.

3   Complete by stitch-in-a-ditch method.

Closed cuffs (Figure 21)

Do not machine sleeve seam for this method.

1   Prepare cuff as before and sew, right sides together, to the base of the sleeve.

31

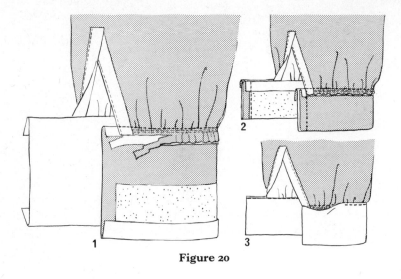

Figure 20

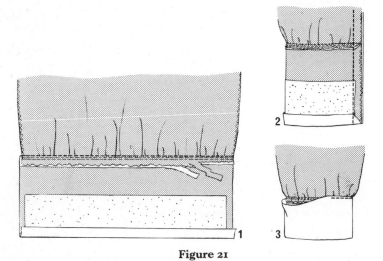

Figure 21

2 Machine sleeve seam and cuff together in one. Trim seams, mitre corners and turn through.

3 Complete by stitch-in-a-ditch method.

ELASTIC CUFFS AND WAISTBANDS (Figure 22)

Method 1

1 The illustrated stretch zig-zag stitches are excellent for machine stitching elastic.

2 First measure the comfortable amount of elastic needed, then stitch into place. Always stretch the elastic to fit the area as you machine. This will gather the area as it goes.

3 Stitch the seam all in one, as shown.

Method 2

This is a quick way of inserting a waistband or enclosed cuff.

1 First measure the length needed, as before, and stitch the elastic into a circle. A square stitched with zig-zag stitches is very strong. Put the circle of the garment inside the circle of elastic and fold over the seam, wrong sides together. Machine into place, stretching the elastic as you go.

2 The illustration shows a skirt with a waistband inserted in this way.

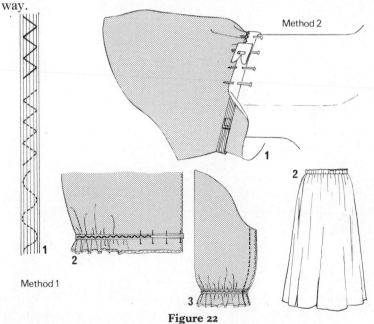

Figure 22

33

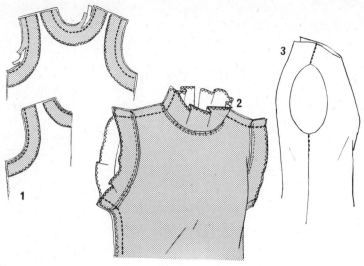

Figure 23

FACINGS

Method 1 (Figure 23)

1 Stitch arm and neck facing into place, right sides together, on individual backs and front.

2 Turn garments to wrong side and stitch side seams and shoulder seams with facings, in one operation. Trim away seams and press into place.

3 Stitch-in-a-ditch method will hold the facings in place across the shoulders and down side seams.

Method 2 (Figure 24)

All-in-one, sleeveless facings are approached in the following way.

1 Stitch shoulder seams on both garment and facings and, placing right sides together, stitch as shown.

2 Trim seams and clip curves. Pull the left-hand back of the garment through channel under shoulder seam. Repeat with right-hand side.

3 Press neck and armhole seams into place. Stitch side seams and facings as shown in **2** of *Method 1*.

Method 3 (Figure 25)

This method is called 'bagging out' and is used here for a waistcoat.

1 Machine both garment and lining seams. Don't forget to do

34

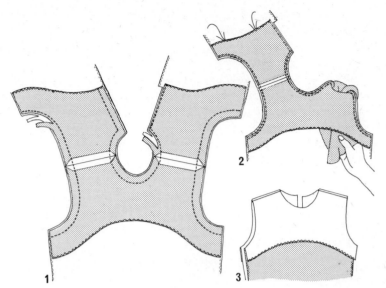

Figure 24

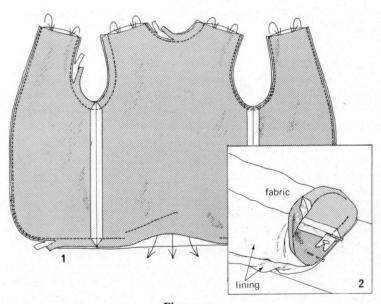

Figure 25

any pockets or top details on the garment first. Lay separate garments, right sides together, and machine as shown. Trim the seams then turn and pull through the gap left in the back hem. Press the waistcoat into shape.

2   Pull one matching front and back shoulder, back out of the gap in the hem and place the armhole seams exactly together, fabric to one side, lining to the other. Stitch the two tubes together, working carefully round. Repeat with the other shoulder seam and return shoulder seams to right side and stitch back hem into place.

Method 4 (not illustrated)
Jacket linings can also be 'bagged out', but the approach is slightly different. Jackets usually have their front and back neck facings in the same fabric as the jacket. With a collarless jacket you could economize on expensive fabric by taking the lining to the front edge as with the waistcoat in *Method 3*.

For jackets with self facings use one of two methods:

1   Machine jacket and lining shells to final stage. Jacket must have collar and facings attached and sleeve and bottom hems completed. Now machine lining and jacket, right sides together, right round outer facing edge and then turn back into position inside jacket and slip stitch by hand into place. (See Phase 4, jacket plan, for illustration.)

2   Cut the lining length shorter by the depth of the jacket hem, but leave a seam allowance. Complete jacket and lining shells, but stitch the upper collar and facing unit to the lining *not* the jacket. Now machine the two garments together, with right sides together, all round the outer edge, leaving a gap in the back hem area through which to pull the jacket to its finished state, as in the waistcoat, *Method 3*.

GATHERING (Figure 26)

1   Here is another way of running a gathering thread. This is particularly good for very heavy fabric that can easily snap an ordinary machine thread. Zig-zag stitch over cord, button-hole twist, or even string for real heavies. Draw up as illustrated.

2   This machine foot will actually gather for you while stitching the gathers to your garment or binding. The amount of gather is dependent on the length of stitch—the longer the stitch the tighter the gather. This method requires a bit of practice to achieve an even gather, especially as the top fabric can slip out of the foot.

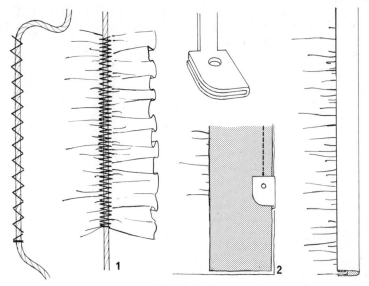

Figure 26

Counteract this by gently pulling towards the right-hand side of the foot as you sew.

HEMS (Figure 27)

1 *Rolled hem* The foot illustrated is available for all types of machines. It sews narrow hems such as those found on linen handkerchiefs. Before you begin, shallow mitre any corner of your work and press the first very narrow fold in place. Set machine to a small straight stitch. Fold the work again in another narrow fold and sew a few stitches in from the corner, without threading the fabric into the roll. Now carefully thread your fabric into the roll and machine the hem. Hold the fabric taut and straight to feed into the roll. If you need to turn a corner, finish the edge completely, remove fabric and begin again, as before, on the new side. *Practise* this one!

2 *Shell edging* The foot for this looks the same as the hemmer, but is in fact for a swing-needle machine. It produces a delicate shell edge for lingerie and light, pretty hems. Use the same method as for **1** but set stitch settings for a medium zig-zag. Different stitch widths alter the size of the pattern.

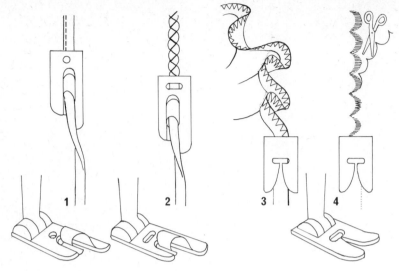

Figure 27

3 *Lettuce* For the lettuce hem you will only need a simple zig-zag stitch foot. This edge looks attractive on stretch jerseys and knits. Press a narrow hem, 9 mm ($\frac{3}{8}$ in), in place and set the machine to a medium zig-zag stitch. The secret of the rippled edge is to gently stretch the fabric as you stitch. Do test this hem first to get the right amount of stretch and stitch.

4 *Scallop* It is possible to do this last type of hem on a semi-automatic machine, but it takes considerable skill to keep the pattern even. Large scallops, about 5 cm (2 in) across, are cut into shape first then stitched round. Fully automatic machines usually have a small delicate scallop pattern in their automatic stitch range. Nothing is easier than this design for lingerie and table linen. Your own instruction book will show you how to set the machine.

LEATHER

Making leather garments can be a tricky business, the cost of the material itself is daunting even to an experienced dressmaker. To help you here are a few tips:

1 Always use a wedge-shaped leather-needle to slice the stitches through the leather and a strong thread—mercerized cotton no 40 is ideal.

2 A simple design will pay dividends in leather and it is wise to make a cotton mock-up for fitting and transferring all the alterations to the paper pattern, before cutting out the leather.

3 Never pin leather. Use adhesive tape to hold the garment while you machine.

4 If you plan to sew with leather a great deal, the special sewing feet with rollers, designed to glide over the leather surface, will be a great help.

PLACKETS

Method 1 (Figure 28)

This is the simplest of all placket openings.

1 Snip an opening in the sleeve, 2.5 cm (1 in) wide and 16 mm ($\frac{5}{8}$ in) deep.

2 Fold over twice and machine.

3 Stitch the sleeve up ready for the cuff

4 Attach cuff and finish from the outside.

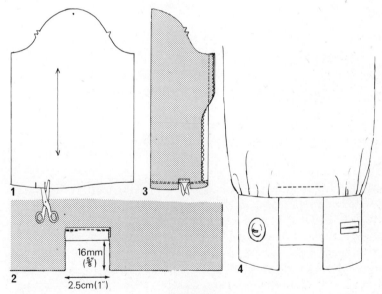

Figure 28

39

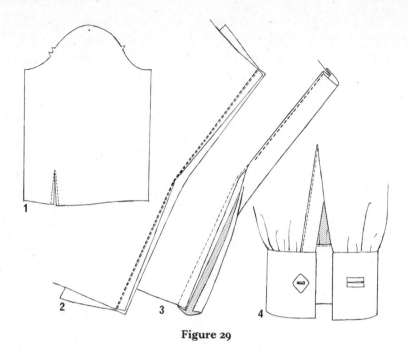

Figure 29

Method 2 (Figure 29)
This method gives a deeper opening.
1   Stay-stitch the split.
2   Open the split to its widest extent and sew a bias strip along.
3   Fold over bias strip and machine into place, just over original stitches.
4   Attach cuff and finish from the outside.
Note   This can be used for various openings, e.g. neck, waist.

PVC

Plastics, like leather, are difficult to sew. They tend to stick on the throat plate and cause stitch problems. A drop of oil spread over the plate and foot base helps, or perhaps the investment in a special sewing foot. There is a Teflon-coated foot especially made to overcome this sticky problem. A normal sharp needle and no 50 mercerized cotton thread are just right. Remember to treat plastics like leather and use adhesive tape to hold the pieces together.

40

SHIRRING

The following super-quick method of sewing elastic is so useful when sewing children's clothes. First wind the bobbin with shirring elastic by hand. Cheap elastic causes problems, so always buy the best. This process can be done either before the side seams are sewn, as for elastic cuffs on page 33, or in the round when the dress is complete. Set your machine to a long, straight stitch and start the first row of stitching. Reverse a few stitches at the beginning of the line just as you would normally, this anchors the elastic firmly. Finish the end of the line in the same way. The shirring will pucker the fabric as you sew. It will help in sewing each succeeding line to pull the fabric taut to ensure that you are sewing on a flat smooth surface. Alternatively, use gathering method 1, Figure 26, on page 37.

SLEEVE—FLAT INSERTION (Figure 30)

This method is very good for beginners who might be put off by the problems of 'setting in a sleeve'. It can only be used for simple sleeves, and it is not suitable for shirts or cuffed sleeves.

1   Draw up the gathering threads to take up the ease on the sleeve head or top. Lay and pin the sleeve head in place on top of the open armhole. Be careful to match the notches. Now machine stitch around the head.

2   Machine stitch the side seam and sleeve in one operation.

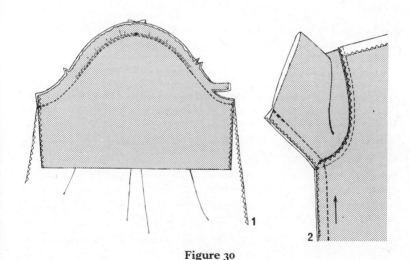

Figure 30

41

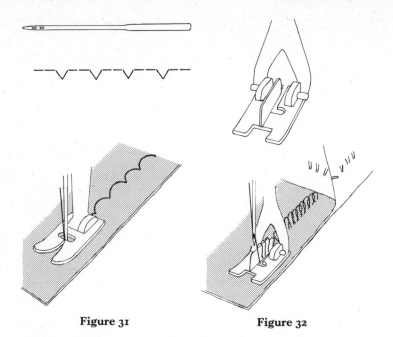

Figure 31 **Figure 32**

TACKING (Figure 31)

If you have a swing-needle machine it is possible to fit a special needle which will do this task. Set your machine to blind stitch with a wide zig-zag and a long straight stitch setting. The needle should also be set to the left. Thread up the top eye of the needle and proceed to sew as normal. Don't forget to allow for the left-hand needle setting when tacking your seam.

TAILOR'S TACKING (Figure 32)

This special foot will make a loose, looped stitch for tailor's tacks. Set your machine for zig-zag stitch with the longest possible straight stitch. It may be necessary to loosen your top tension to make a looser stitch. Having finished the machining, ease the fabric apart and snip between the threads.

TOP-STITCHING FOR DECORATION

One of the most professional finishes on a garment is beautiful, neat lines of top-stitching. It is well worth practising to achieve good results. The kind of finish you get depends on what thread you use. Colour, shine and thickness of stitch all play a part in the final look of the top-stitching. If you want to make a feature of thick, glossy top-stitching choose a special button thread. For a simpler matt finish use the thread with which you are sewing your garment. All threads can be used single or double for top-stitching. To use double thread wind up two more bobbins and use on top of each other on the thread spool, thread up the needle normally, using the two threads as one. When sewing with button thread it is often wiser to leave the bobbin wound with your usual sewing thread as button thread can make stitching too bulky if used underneath as well. Lengthen the stitch to the longest possible. *Do not* begin sewing in the normal way, ie reversing to hold, but follow the method set out in Phase 2, tips and techniques **12**. If your machine has a device to set the needle to the left or right of centre, do use this to help stitching accuracy, as the foot will ride firmly over the fabric while the needle sews closer to the edge. Don't forget the decorative possibilities that a double or treble needle can give to top-stitching.

UNDERSTITCHING (Figure 33)

This is the reverse of top-stitching and is definitely not meant to be seen. Its function is to hold facings and collar edges in place. The illustration shows clearly how this is done, but make sure you trim

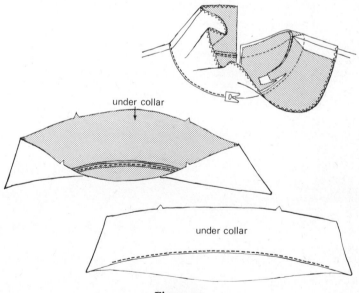

Figure 33

43

the seam allowance underneath *before* you stitch the seam allowance and facing together.

Waistbands (Figure 34)

There are two ways of approaching the standard waistband. Method 1 has practically invisible stitching when finished; Method 2 has a line of top-stitching at the waist and is the faster method. For either method attach interfacing and press seam allowance in place to prepare waistband.

Method 1

1 Begin by stitching the prepared waistband, right sides together.

2 Turn it to the inside of the garment and stitch into place from the front by stitch-in-a-ditch method.

Method 2

1 Reverse this process and start by sewing the waistband to the inside of the skirt, waistband right side to skirt wrong side.

2 Turn the band over to the front and top-stitch in place as shown.

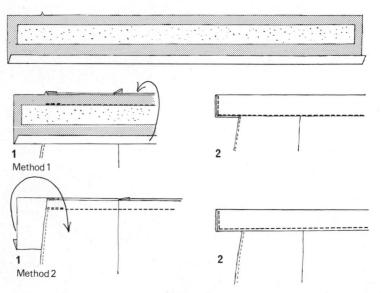

Figure 34

44

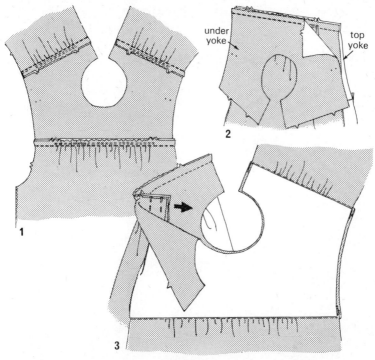

Figure 35

Yokes (Figure 35)

This method eliminates hand stitching under-yokes into place.

1 Stitch top yoke into position back and front, as usual.

2 Machine under-yoke at the back, as shown, stitching just above the first machine line.

3 Sew one side of the front yoke by reaching inside through the neck and sewing along from the armhole towards the neck. Repeat on the other side of the front yoke.

Zips

Method 1 (Figure 36)

1 Fit your machine with the special zipper or cording foot which is designed to allow the needle to sew very close to the zip or cord. Position the needle to the left side, and having pressed the seam flat, turn the zip over and place it with the tab at the top of the opening. Pin to hold and machine as close to the teeth as the zip will

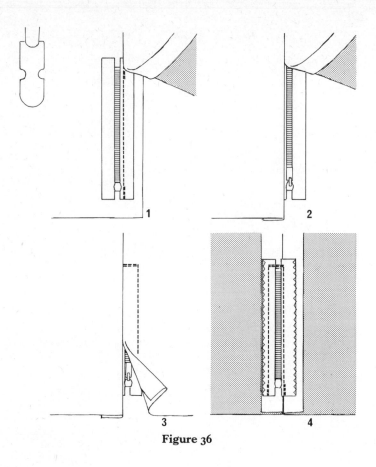

Figure 36

allow. Remember to start and finish with reverse stitch to strengthen. Run the slider down to check the freedom of movement.

2 Turn the zip right side upwards. This will conceal the stitching.

3 Move the needle over to the right side of the foot for this next step. Fold over the right side of the seam opening and butt the two seam edges together. Pin into position and machine stitch 6 mm ($\frac{1}{4}$ in) from the teeth, working on the right side of the fabric. Turn the corner at the base of the zip and machine twice across the bottom for strength.

4 Another line of stitching around the edge of the zip tape attaching it to the seam allowance will also add strength.

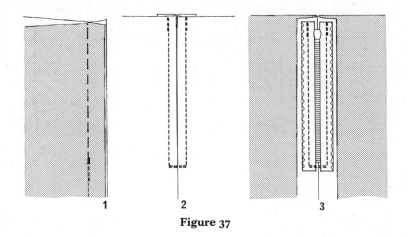

Figure 37

Method 2 (Figure 37)

1   Loosely tack the opening of the seam together and press flat.

2   Lay the garment on a flat surface whilst positioning the zip with its tabs butting to the top edge of the opening. Roll the zip down the seam with its teeth centred *exactly* over the seam opening. Pin to hold. Position needle to the right of the foot and machine round the zip 6 mm ($\frac{1}{4}$ in) from the teeth, working on the right side.

3   Finish inside as **4** in *Method 1*.

Phase 4
Making up garments

Most home dressmakers will tack and fit, then machine the body of the garment, add the collar, facings and the pockets and then set in the sleeves before finally finishing off seam edges and hems. This method is perfect when you are experimenting with a new and difficult pattern, or if you gain pleasure and relaxation from producing your own clothes. But everyone, grown-ups and children alike, needs basic everyday garments which can be made very quickly from simple patterns. Using basic patterns for your family's wardrobe does not become monotonous, as the range of fabrics and trimmings available to vary the picture is enormous. Speeding up production of everyday clothes will leave you more time to sew the interesting extras you need and more money to buy lovely accessories for your new wardrobe!

Instant dressmaking

There are three magic 'ingredients' for instant dressmaking:
1   Rearrange the sequence of putting the garment together.
2   Never tack—use pins to prepare each stage for machining.
3   Your iron will be invaluable, not only to finish off work but also to prepare it for the machine.

1   You might well have found that fitting a patch pocket to the front of a dress that has already been sewn together is not easy—but to complete that process before the dress has been constructed is simple. That, in a nutshell, is what you will be doing—completing the details on each piece before it is finally joined into the whole garment. The following basic work plans will show the construction sequence to follow. As you gain experience in sewing in this way you will be able to adapt it for each new pattern you undertake; you will see construction problems before they occur and be able to plan ahead to avoid them.

2   The 'no-tacking' method was first mentioned in Phase 2, tips and techniques **10.** The sewing needle very rarely breaks while stitching over the pins, and the time and energy saved by using this method compensates for the occasional broken needle. Don't over-pin a seam. The top two edges obviously need holding in position, thereafter follow down the seam about every 15 cm (6 in). Very occasionally the two layers of fabric will slide against each other and after machining finish unevenly. Don't despair, if the discrepancy is less than 2.5 cm (1 in), no-one will know if you neatly snip off the surplus.

3   It really helps to have your iron on and the ironing surface close at hand while you are sewing. If there are small children near, make sure that the hot iron is always firmly held in a heat-proof stand to prevent accidents.

Please do not press your dressmaking as you would the family washing. It is quite a different art. The light passing strokes you use for everyday ironing are not strong enough to hold or flatten your sewing. Pressing is just as the word says—you 'press' gently with a whole iron on one place for a few seconds, preferably with the aid of steam. Both a damp and a dry cotton cloth are essential when you are pressing. If you are worried that your fabric will shine after pressing, place the dry cloth between the fabric and the damp cloth. Pressing gently with the point of the iron will open up seams and fiddly corners ready for the heavier pressing if necessary. If you have chosen a pile fabric, such as velvet, cord or velour, press with the right side of the fabric on top of either a soft towel or a spare piece of your fabric. The two piles will absorb each other and prevent flattening. For more information on pressing, the book called *Pressing*, in this series, is invaluable.

Work plans

The following plans will show a quicker sequence of construction for a dress, blouse, jacket, skirt and trousers. The methods of machining (ie how to make a cuff or set in a sleeve) are not discussed. You will find speedy machining methods for these details in Phase 3. The sewing is arranged in blocks of work, after which you press all the sewing, then proceed to the next 'block'. This saves time wasted by getting up to press each individual piece! 'Prepare hem or seam' means to press into the desired depth before machining. This makes for more accurate stitching.

Style : Sheath dress with short, set-in sleeves and a zip in the back seam. Patch pockets on front skirt.

Block 1   *Prepare*

1   Cut out all pattern pieces before you start.

2   It will save time if you use the snip-and-chalk method of transferring pattern marks from paper pattern to fabric. Make small scissor snips within the seamline where balance marks occur. Then pierce the end of the dart, or whatever point is required, with a pin. Roll the pattern back and chalk the pin mark. Turn the fabric over and chalk the pin mark on the other side.

3   Iron on fusible interfacings, or tack on lawn interfacings, to collars, cuffs, and facings. Press under the seams of patch pockets ready for top-stitching.

Block 2 (Figure 38)   *Machine*

1   Stay stitch if necessary (see Phase 2, tips and techniques **11**).

2   Stitch all darts.

3   Finish all side seam edges, shoulder seam edges and facing edges.

4   Top-stitch pockets into place on front of dress skirt.

5   Stitch together collar and neck facings.

6   Stitch back seam ready for zip.

Block 3   *Press*

Press all the sewing, seams and darts.

Block 4 (Figure 39)   *Machine*

1   Insert back zip.

2   Stitch shoulder seams.

3   Stitch collar and neck facings into place. (Can be done in one operation.)

4   'Stitch in a ditch' for neck facing—shoulder seam under collar.

5   Stitch a gathering line around sleeve head.

6   Stitch sleeve head into armhole. (There are two ways of setting in sleeves. This method is good for simple sleeves with simple finished hems such as elastic insertion or plain turned hems. A buttoned cuff or frilled hem is handled more easily on separate sleeves. See blouse plan for this second method.)

7   Neaten armhole seam by stitching the two edges together with zig-zag stitch.

8   Stitch dress side seams and sleeve seam in one operation.

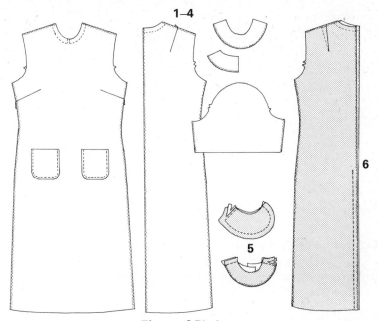

Figure 38 Block 2

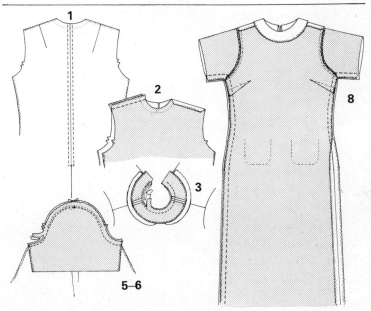

Figure 39 Block 4

Block 5   *Press*

1   Press all sewing—seams, collar etc.

2   Press dress and sleeve hems ready to stitch.

Block 6   *Machine*

Machine all hems by either top-stitching or blind hemming.

BLOUSE PLAN

Style : Shirt-collared blouse with yoke shoulders and gathered back and front. Long sleeves with buttoned cuff.

Block 1   *Prepare*

As for dress plan.

Block 2 (Figure 40)   *Machine*

1   Stay stitch if necessary.

2   Turn back front facing and top-stitch in place. Alternatively stitch on separate facing if the design of the pattern requires it.

3   Stitch gathering lines on front and back body pieces and sleeve head.

4   Stitch yoke on to front and back body pieces.

5   Stitch on under yoke as shown on page 45.

6   Neaten side seams, facing edges and sleeve seams.

7   Stitch collar together.

Block 3   *Press*

Press all sewing, seams etc.

Block 4 (Figure 41)   *Machine*

1   Stitch collar into place.

2   Stitch blouse side seams and sleeve seams.

3   Finish sleeve hem with button cuff. (See pages 31 and 32 for quick methods.)

4   Insert sleeve.

5   Neaten armhole seam.

Block 5   *Press*

1   Press all sewing.

2   Prepare hem for top-stitching.

3   Mark button-holes.

Block 6   *Machine*

1   Machine hem, either by top-stitching or blind-hemming.

2   Machine button-holes and buttons in place.

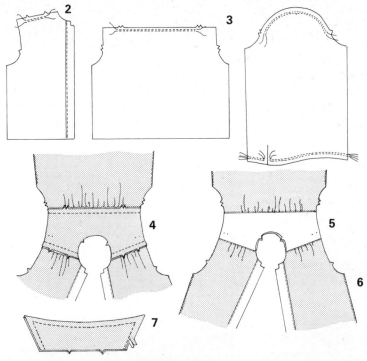

Figure 40 Block 2

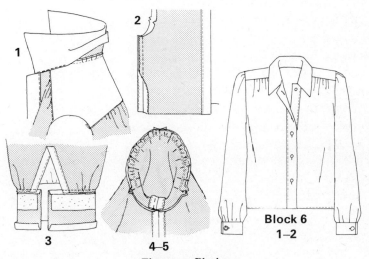

Figure 41 Block 4

Style : Lined, blazer jacket with collar revers, flap pockets, and raglan sleeves. Bound buttonholes.

Block 1   *Prepare*

1   Cut out all jacket and lining pieces and transfer all pattern markings.
2   Iron on interfacings or tack on suitable interfacing for collar, jacket front, sleeve hem and flap pockets.

Block 2 (Figure 42)   *Machine*

1   Stay stitch as necessary. Stitch tailor's tape on dolman armhole seams for strength.
2   Stitch all darts on sleeve and jacket.
3   Stitch and turn pocket flaps.
4   Stitch all bound button-holes to the stage before attaching and cutting through facing.
5   Stitch together neck and front facing.

Block 3   *Press*

Press darts and pocket flaps, button-holes and neck facings.

Block 4 (Figure 43)   *Machine*

1   Top-stitch pocket flaps (optional).
2   Sew on pocket and pocket flaps.
3   Stitch top collar to neck facing.
4   Stitch dolman sleeves into armholes.
5   Stitch under-collar into place.

Block 5   *Press*

Press top and under-collar seams, sleeve seams and pockets.

Block 6 (Figure 44)   *Machine*

1   Stitch facing and top collar on to jacket.
2   Stitch jacket side seams and sleeve in one.
3   Sew jacket lining together: sleeve dart; sleeve to lining front and back body; side and sleeve seam.

Block 7   *Press*

1   Press the collar and facing into place.
2   Press jacket lining.
3   Prepare jacket and sleeve hems for machining.

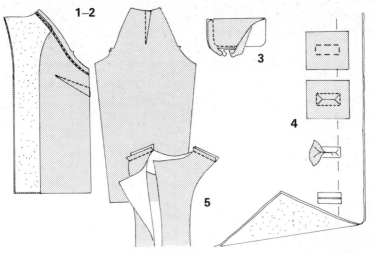

Figure 42 Block 2

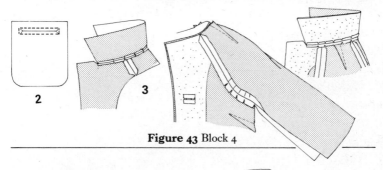

Figure 43 Block 4

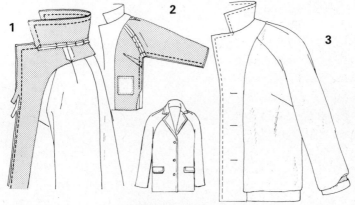

Figure 44 Block 6

Block 8 *Machine*

1 Blind-hem jacket and sleeve hems.
2 Top-stitch collar and jacket front edge.
3 Stitch lining into jacket (method shown on page 36).

Block 9 *Hand stitching*

1 Cut, turn and sew facings around button-holes.
2 Slip-stitch sleeve linings to sleeve hem.

Skirt plan

Style : Unlined skirt with soft gathers at front waist, darts in the back. Zip in back seam.

Block 1 *Prepare*

1 Cut out and mark all pattern pieces.
2 Press waistband in half, attach petersham or interfacing and then press one edge of the waistband over 16 mm ($\frac{5}{8}$ in) seam allowance.

Block 2 (Figure 45) *Machine*

1 Finish all seam edges.
2 Stitch back darts and back seams.
3 Stitch gathering line at front waistline.

Block 3 *Press*

Press seams and darts.

Block 4 (Figure 46) *Machine*

1 Insert zip.
2 Stitch side seams.
3 Stitch petersham on to waistband.
4 Stitch one side of waistband on inside of skirt.
5 Fold waistband over and top-stitch into place.
6 Neaten hem edge.

Block 5 *Press*

1 Press seams and waistband.
2 Prepare hem.

Block 6 *Machine*

Blind-stitch hem on machine.

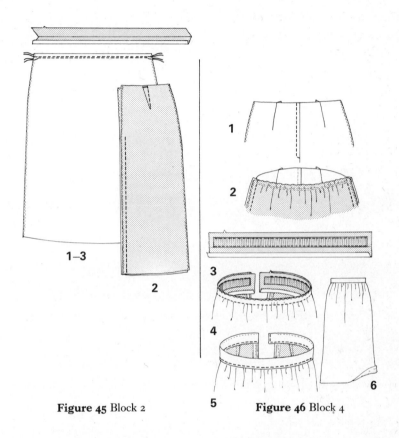

Figure 45 Block 2

Figure 46 Block 4

Style : Straight trousers, darted in the waist. Pockets let into side seams. Front seam zip.

Block 1   *Prepare*
1   Cut out and mark all pattern pieces.
2   Press waistband in half and then one edge over as in skirt plan.

Block 2 (Figure 47)   *Machine*
1   Finish seam edges of leg seams, crotch and outer edge of pockets.
2   Stitch all darts.
3   Stitch back and front inside leg seams together on each leg.
4   Stitch crotch seams together right through, leaving opening for the zip.
5   Stitch four pocket pieces into position on side seams.
6   Stitch petersham into waistband.

Block 3   *Press*
Press all sewing.

Block 4 (Figure 48)   *Machine*
1   Insert zip.
2   Turn trousers to stitch outside leg seam.
3   Stitch side seams and pockets in one operation.
4   Stitch waistband into place *inside* trousers.
5   Top-stitch band on to front trouser to finish off.
6   Finish bottom edge of trouser legs.

Block 5   *Press*
1   Press all sewing so far.
2   Press up leg hem.

Block 6   *Machine*
Blind-stitch or top-stitch trouser hems.

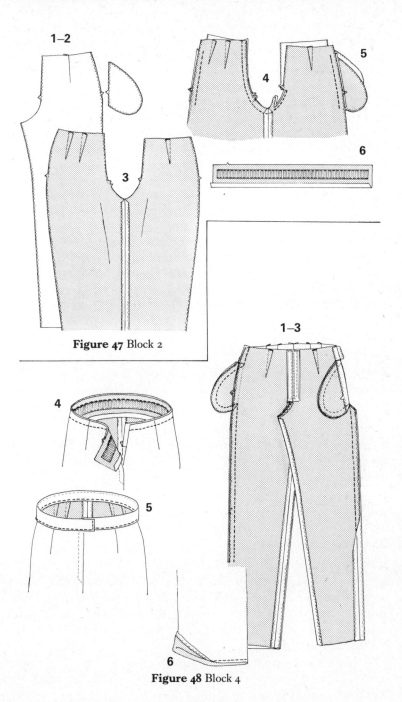

1–2

3

4

5

6

Figure 47 Block 2

1–3

4

5

6

Figure 48 Block 4

Phase 5

Machine maintenance

The maintenance of your sewing machine is just as important as learning how to use it. No household appliance should be required to work at peak performance without being cared for.

If you sew infrequently, never store your machine without cleaning and oiling it first. Regular dressmakers should clean and oil after every project.

Equipment

1 *Small paint brush*   To brush out dust and fluff from awkward corners.

2 *Oil*   Choose a good, light oil specially formulated for sewing machines.

3 *Screwdrivers*   Your machine should be supplied with all the neccessary tools. But in the event, as with older machines, of these having been lost, measure the groove in the screw heads that you will need to remove and buy the correct size screwdriver.

4 *Paper tissues*   For mopping up oil and for dusting.

Cleaning and oiling

1   Unplug electric machine before oiling.

2   Consult your instruction manual about where to oil. Try not to over oil as this can cause just as many problems as not oiling at all! If you have a new machine you may find that oiling is not necessary as oil has been sealed into the relevant parts of the machine by the manufacturer.

3   Dismantle the bobbin area if possible and brush out accumulated fluff with your paint brush.

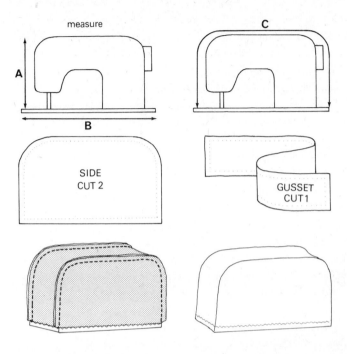

measure

A

B

C

SIDE
CUT 2

GUSSET
CUT 1

4 Dust the surfaces and around the back of the motor.

5 If you are storing the machine leave the needle lowered into a scrap of folded cotton. This will absorb any excess oil.

6 If your machine is stored on a work surface and in regular use a cotton cover will protect it from dust and save the bother of a heavy case for storage. Follow the instructions for making a cover in Figure 49.

Fault finding

Many sewing machine faults are actually due to *you*! It is very easy to be absent-minded when setting up or threading your machine. So when a problem occurs run through the following check list before you panic!

Fault check list I—Elementary

1 Is socket switched on?

2 Is every plug in and connected properly?

3 Are bobbin and needle correctly threaded and fitted in position? Needle must be inserted correctly.

4 Have you chosen the right thread and needles for the project?

5 Is the needle blunt or snagged?

6 Is the foot attached properly?

7 Are the dials positioned correctly for your chosen stitch?

8 Is the hand wheel release tightened?

9 Is the drop feed set to darn?

10 Is the machine clear of fluff and recently oiled?

If your machine is still giving you trouble, look next at what kind of fault is involved.

1 *Electrical* The machine has little or no electric power.

2 *Stitch malfunction* The stitches are badly formed, loose or skipped. The bobbin thread is knotted or the fabric puckered.

Fault check list II—Electrical

1 Have you checked list I first?

2 No power? Change the fuse in the plug.

3 Electricity functions, but machine won't sew:

a) Electric presser foot has become obstructed and cannot be pressed down fully.

b) Electrical connections are faulty because the plugs from the motor and electrical presser foot are too loose to hold in place. Try adhesive tape to keep them bedded in properly for the project in hand, then take the machine to your service agent.

If the fault is anything other than one of the minor faults mentioned, take the machine to your service repair agent.

Fault check list III—Stitch malfunction

All too often home dressmakers blame the 'tension' for bad stitching. More harm is done by fiddling with tension dials than by any other fault. On modern machines the tension is pre-set at the factory to cover every possibility, so *don't touch!* Only after all else fails is it wise to alter the tensions. To find if the needle and bobbin tensions are compatible with each other try this quick test: thread up the machine completely, ready to sew. Now gently draw the bobbin and needle threads towards you. If they both glide out at an equal rate, there is no problem. If one or other comes too fast or in slow jerks, consult your instruction manual on altering tension.

1 Have you checked list I first?

2 *Slipped stitches :*
   a) Are you using a blunt needle?
   b) Are you using cheap or unsuitable thread for the project?
   c) Are the upper thread guides clear and clean?

3 *Needle breaks :*
   a) Check needle position (List I, 3).
   b) Is the needle bent and missing the needle plate hole?

Useful tip
Always take the finished work out towards the back of the foot, carefully drawing the threads after it. The needle can bend if this is done roughly. It will also help if, when stitching very thick, tough fabrics, you try not to pull or push the work when the needle is in the fabric as this can also bend needles. A pitted needle plate must be repolished by a service agent.

4 *Upper thread breaks :* Only after testing needle and thread as in list I do you alter the tension.

5 *Lower thread breaks :* As above

6 *Knotting bobbin threads :*
   a) Start the seam correctly (Phase 2, tips and techniques 5).
   b) Is stitch length set at 0?
   c) Is needle presser foot lowered?

7 *Seam puckers :*
   a) Check Phase 2, tips and techniques 9, thread and needle guide, to see if you have chosen correctly for your project.
   b) Is stitch length too small?
   c) Does the fabric need a zig-zag stitch?

Useful tip
Some fabrics are best stretched gently as they feed under the needle presser foot.
   Press the seam well and leave to hang for a while.